ALMOST THERE

PHILIP J. GENTLESK

ALMOST THERE

PHILIP J. GENTLESK

Printed in the United States of America.
ISBN-13:
979-8-9906415-2-5 Paperback
979-8-9906415-3-2 Hardcover

Royal Crest Publishing
Waxhaw, North Carolina

Royal Crest
PUBLISHING

CONTENTS

CHAPTER ONE

WHERE DID WE COME FROM AND WHERE ARE WE GOING?

These are questions that every thinking person would like to have answered.

Certainly, there are some people who don't care how they got here, or where they are going when their life on earth is over. But the fact that you are reading this book tells me that you are not one of these people.

The first thing you need to know is that you are not here by accident. Your existence is not the result of an accidental collision of various chemicals, or the product of a cosmic explosion somewhere in outer space.

Instead, you were created by an intelligent being who knows your name, loves you more than you can understand, and wants you to spend eternity with him in the paradise He has prepared for you. Yes, I am talking about God, the One who is the author of all life. As the Bible says, **"GOD CREATED MAN IN HIS OWN IMAGE, IN THE IMAGE OF GOD HE CREATED HIM; MALE AND FEMALE HE CRE-ATED THEM." (GENESIS 1:27.)**

So, this is where we came from. We are individual creations, built with care by a loving God. We are not a random collection of atoms that will be blown away by the wind after we die.

Back in the late 19th century, a theory called "spontaneous generation' was popular throughout Europe and the United States. This theory stated that it was possible for life to spring up spontaneously from non-living material. For example, suppose you came upon a dead bird that had been lying on the ground for a while and took a close look at it. Where did all those maggots come from? Some speculated that they had generated spontaneously. We know now that those little "worms" came from fly eggs that were deposited onto the dead bird's carcass. Spontaneous generation was also said to create mice from bread crumbs, fleas from dust, and many other types of small animals and insects.

Spontaneous generation was completely discredited, largely through the work of Luis Pasteur.   Today, nobody believes that spontaneous generation is a real thing. And yet, millions upon millions of people believe in the theory of evolution, which holds that all life, including human life, was created by a random collision of chemicals. It just does not make sense.

GOD GAVE YOU FREE WILL.

You may not agree with what I'm saying and that is your right. When God created human beings, he gave us free will in order that we can make our own choices. Man is a free moral agent, to do and proclaim anything he believes, even if what he believes is wrong. And yet, wrong choices carry consequences, and can even lead you to jail if you break the law.

Here are just a few of the terrible disasters wrong choices have led to: The Russian Revolution of 1905, Genocide in West Africa (Namibia), the Spanish Flu, two World Wars, a drastic increase in the divorce rate, homosexuality as an accepted way of life, terrorism, the spread of drugs, materialism, extreme weather, earthquakes, and the development of Artificial Intelligence.

Artificial Intelligence (AI) refers to computers that simulate human intelligence in order to perform tasks and solve problems. In our lifetime, AI will alter our world more than the development of electricity. This is a bold statement, but I believe it to be true. Twenty years ago, did anyone see that social media would lead to young girls cutting themselves, or whole towns being overrun by hoodlums, or even these tent cities exploding everywhere to accommodate the tremendous influx of immigrants. The most chilling thing associated with AI is that it is very hard to keep up with its minute-by-minute advancements. AI is all about machines having the ability to 'learn on their own so they can play a major role in healthcare, finance, and transportation.' These intelligent machines literally make decisions that a human brain may make! Where all this leads to is the 'Battle of Armageddon,' The Tribulation period and the return of Christ.

FAITH LIGHTS THE WAY IN A DARK WORLD

One very important thing to remember is, "What you believe, (i.e. your belief system) will determine your future." If you really know God, your behavior will reflect that belief. God's mechanism for growth is faith. In Hebrews 11:6, the Bible says, **"AND WITHOUT FAITH IT IS IMPOSSIBLE TO PLEASE HIM, FOR HE WHO COMES TO GOD MUST BELIEVE THAT HE IS AND THAT HE IS A REWARDER OF THOSE WHO SEEK HIM."**

HOW DO YOU INCREASE YOUR FAITH?

Before we answer that question, let's look at what weakens your faith. Any traumatic event in your life will cause you to question whether life is worthwhile. Anxiety, depression, loss of a family member or mental health issues will cause doubt to creep into your head. In such cases I always encourage people to read 1 Thessalonian: 5:18: **"REJOICE**

ALWAYS, PRAY CONTINUALLY, GIVE THANKS IN ALL CIRCUM-STANCES; FOR THIS IS GOD'S WILL FOR YOU IN CHRIST JESUS." Therefore, increasing our faith requires the desire to know more about Jesus. We must learn about His love, His mercy, His Justice, and how we can get to know Him.

Start by reading your Bible. How did you meet your husband or wife? You did it by communicating. You got to know each other's families. You learned about each other's likes and dislikes. It is the same way with a relationship with Christ. Your problem may be that because you can't see Him, you think He is not real. But John 20:29 says, **"BECAUSE YOU HAVE SEEN ME, HAVE YOU NOW BELIEVED, BLESSED ARE THEY WHO DID NOT SEE, AND YET BELIEVED."** In order to believe, you must have evidence. Faith is learning to trust what you know is true. Therefore, biblical faith is based on evidence.

In his article written in April 2020, Mr. George Sinclair stated, "There are four ancient biographies of Jesus, all of which were written by eyewitnesses. They all state Jesus indeed rose from the dead. These biographies were supplemented by eyewitness letters. These letters claim Jesus was crucified and on the third day rose from the dead."

He goes on to talk about Jewish writer and historian, Josephus, and pagan writers such as Thallos, Pliny the younger, Suetonius, etc., all of whom testified about the life and death of Christ. He explains that many eyewitnesses who saw the resurrection were killed because they would not recant what they knew to be true. They died because they knew that the resurrection was true.

He further explains that the Apostle John wrote two books. The first was the real story of Jesus (Gospel of John). The second was the Book of Revelation, which is Christ's telling mankind what the future will bring. In his Gospel, John gives us historical evidence for the resurrection: The grave was empty, grave clothes were neatly folded and left behind, the 3,000-pound stone that enclosed the grave was rolled aside, Jesus body was never found. This grave was guarded by Roman soldiers, and it is a known fact that these soldiers were given money to keep their mouths shut regarding the missing Jesus (in other words they were to keep quiet about His missing body).

Finally, not counting Paul, there were eleven recorded times that Jesus appeared to people, proving His resurrection.[1]

1 Corinthians 15:6 tells us, **"THEN HE APPEARED TO MORE THAN FIVE HUNDRED BRETHREN AT ONE TIME, MOST OF WHOM ARE STILL ALIVE, THOUGH SOME HAVE FALLEN ASLEEP."**

In determining the validity of the above, consider Aristotle. How do you know he lived? Was he fictional or real? You never met him or saw him, and neither did anyone else in the modern era. In other words, all we have to go on are words, either from his peers or himself. He indeed lived and died. He was born in 384 B.C. and died in 322. He was trained first in Medicine. Then, in 367, he was sent to Athens, to study philosophy with Plato. He was taught that we learn moral virtue through habit and practice rather than through reasoning.

The same can be said for Jesus. The primary difference being that Jesus spoke the truth 100 percent of the time. All I am saying is that Jesus Christ was born, most likely in the same year that Herod the Great died. Approximately 4 BCE. Why does all this matter? Because most individuals only believe what they can see, touch, or what they read on the internet. It's easier to believe in Star Wars than the Gospel but that's about to change in a very dramatic way.

EVERYTHING IS ABOUT TO CHANGE

Soon--very soon--the message will be loud and clear.

Assume it's the day Jesus returns. You look up and see the creator of all mankind descending on a cloud. Seriously, I want you to close your

---

[1] "A 'concise' evidence for the Resurrection of Jesus" by Rev, Canon George Sinclair, "Anglican Network.ca, April 16, 2020

eyes and imagine this day. Soon, your imagination will be replaced by reality! You realize all you heard from the born-again preachers is true. Your shock is replaced with a question: "Where did all the people go?" Then as it hits you like a brick, you realize the day has come, and you have run out of time. You missed Him the first time because you were too proud or too ashamed to have Jesus (Yeshua) become the captain of your life. Wake-up! Think about it! you are caught in a spiritual battle for your very soul. And the consequences of ignoring the call from Jesus are eternal.

As you reel from the Lord's sudden appearance in the sky, you realize that you have never done a thing to make yourself fit for eternity in heaven. You didn't because you never thought heaven was real. After all, the brilliant Stephen Hawking told you that heaven was a fairy tale.

In an article in the Guardian,[2] Mr. Hawking rejected the idea of life beyond death. According to him we should make good use of our lives now and not spend time worrying about a future that doesn't exist.

Albert Einstein was another brilliant scientist who didn't believe in a personal God or an afterlife. Toward the end of his life, Einstein said he was not an atheist, but preferred being called an agnostic. He also said, "One life is enough for me."

We would all agree that men like Albert Einstein and Stephen Hawking lived one life. Then they died. Where they are right now, we do not know.

But there was another man, named Jesus – the Son of God -- who chose to shed Himself of all His Godliness and become a mortal man in order that He might open the doors to eternal salvation and teach us about the amazing love of God.

If you want to understand what Jesus did for you—and all human kind—consider this: Do you love dogs? Most people do. Well, if you

---

[2] Stephen Hawking, "There is no heaven: it's a fairy story," May 15, 2011

had the choice, would you become a dog yourself to bring salvation to canines everywhere? Would you give up everything you have and are to take all the sins of the dog world upon yourself. Would you become a dog and choose death to save other dogs? I think not.

But now, you have a new perspective on what Jesus did for you.

Let us face the facts. Jesus was a real man, but He was also our creator, God. So basically, God gave God to save man. Why? Because He loves us! We, as humans, cannot conceive of the love that God has for us.

We know that we live in a universe built on laws--such as the law of gravity. What goes up must come down--unless you strap a jet engine on its back. Then what goes up can stay up. So, the law of gravity is not as great as the law of aerodynamics.

Whether we are talking about physical or spiritual laws, the highest law is the law of Love. This law requires man to love as God loves, always looking to help our fellow man, without looking for anything in return. James, the Lord's half-brother, called it "Royal Law." In James 2:8 he wrote, **"ALL THE LAW IS FULFILLED IN ONE WORD, 'IF, HOWEVER, YOU ARE FULFILLING THE ROYAL LAW ACCORDING TO THE SCRIPTURE, "YOU SHALL LOVE YOUR NEIGHBOR AS YOURSELF, YOU ARE DOING WELL."**

GOD LOVES ALL PEOPLE

The bottom line is that God loves you, God loves your neighbor, God loves all men! That is the largest stumbling block for our Muslim brothers and sisters. Allah, according to the Muslim faith, is compassionate and merciful, but only to those who obey him. The relationship between Allah and his creature is one of master and servant and not father and son. The Koran does not identify Allah as a Loving Creator.

The Bible tells us that one of the chief attributes of God is His love for His creation. The Koran identifies Allah's chief attribute as his transcendence. Putting it in laymen's words, Allah has no feelings toward mankind. The thinking is that the very idea of Allah having a relationship with men is blasphemous. So, the difference is the god of Muslims loves man only if man keeps all the rules. The Biblical God loves His creation and offers a plan (Jesus Christ) so mankind can find salvation. Allah has no plan but this: Keep the rules and you just might make it!

WHERE DID MAN COME FROM?

The Darwin camp would emphatically say, 'Man' evolved! The key is not what Darwin thought, but what the Lord created. All the veins in your body should be your first clue that you did not just came from some 'Big Bang.'

There is no way your body could have evolved from "nothing" as many scientists say it did. It takes every bit of your will power to believe nonsense like this. You were created by God, and you were created for a purpose. You have meaning in your life on earth, if you want to waste your time by creating your own gods, you have the free will to do this. There are so many "gods" out there: Food, clothes, automobiles, house lust, and one that hits men hardest: sports!

What provokes such addictions in sport? Simply stated, they usually begin with a feeling of low self-esteem. You begin by jogging. Then as time begins to unfold, you add in calisthenics, followed by more miles on your jogging. It becomes a vicious circle where you are pushing yourself all the time. If you don't pay homage to these self-created idols every day you don't feel right. You begin looking at your workout routine as essential to your physical and mental health--which it's not. In 2011, the World Health Organization recognized it as "Behavioral Dependence" (the same as gambling, compulsive shopping, video game addiction, eating disorders, etc. It has been given a name, "bigorexia," in Europe.

Bigorexia has been defined as a compulsive need to work out constantly to produce bigger muscles. No matter how muscular these people may become, they still see themselves as weak and skinny. People with this disorder may spend great amounts of money on ineffective sports supplements or refuse to do anything that does not have to do with working out. They do this to obtain immediate gratification despite the long-term negative consequences on their own personal and social health.

CHAPTER TWO

WHICH WILL YOU CHOOSE — HEAVEN OR HELL?

"... IF SERVING THE LORD SEEMS UNDESIRABLE TO YOU, THEN CHOOSE FOR YOURSELVES THIS DAY WHOM YOU WILL SERVE, WHETHER THE GODS YOUR ANCESTORS SERVED BEYOND THE EUPHRATES, OR THE GODS OF THE AMORITES, IN WHOSE LAND YOU ARE LIVING. BUT AS FOR ME AND MY HOUSEHOLD, WE WILL SERVE THE LORD." (JOSHUA 24:15)

Have you ever wondered what some of the great civilizations of the past thought about life, death and what lies beyond this world? I've discovered that it can be a fascinating study. Consider ancient Egypt, for example. The master builders, responsible or the marvels of the pyramids and the Sphinx, believed that before time was invented, the universe was filled with endless dark waters, called Nun.

In this darkness was a primordial hill known as 'ben-ben' on which there was a great god, 'Ra Atum,' who created himself out of the Nun. He was lonely, so he created life using his magic 'Heka.' It was further believed that the creator god, Amun came from the Nun as the Benny Bird, and then went to the sun city of Heliopolis, where he constructed a nest called Pyramidion, where the Benny was miraculously brought to life from the breath of fire. The Benny became a symbol of immortality and rebirth.

He gave life to two children; Shu (the god of air) and Tefnut (goddess of moisture). The two of them then began creating life and order. They left Ra on the Ben-Ben in the middle of chaos, and when they returned, he shed tears of joy that fertilized the earth. It took a long time to create the heavens. This fable gets even stranger as Shu and Tefnut create Geb (the earth) and Nut (the sky).

Another of the great ancient civilizations, Sumer, gave us things like codes for laws, literature, cuneiform writing, and the creation of beer! What did they believe about heaven or hell? According to Encyclopedia Britannica, the Sumerians believed the afterlife was a rather "shadowy" continuance of life on earth, but whether you had been "good" or "evil" on earth made no impact on how you were treated in the life beyond. The Sumerians believed that the afterlife was centered in a dark cavern below ground where life would continue as it had been on the surface. There certainly wasn't much to look forward to as far as the Sumerians were concerned, but then I suppose there wasn't much to dread either.

Now let's look at one of the oldest religions on earth, Zoroastrianism. Proponents of this religion believed that at the time of death the soul passes over a bridge, at the entrance of which stands the 'daena' (conscience) who can be identified as a maiden. The good see a dignified, beautiful woman, as they pass over the House of Songs, while the bad are caught by an ugly witch, and then fall as demons into the dark ravine, known as the House of Lies.

Which of the above "ways to heaven" would you choose? Or perhaps you would opt for the Hindu afterlife program. Most Hindus believe that upon death their atman (soul) is reborn into a different body. They further believe that the soul may enter Swarga Loka, which means heaven or good kingdom, or Narak (a hellish realm) for a period before rebirth.

They also believe in karma, which means, primarily, that what goes around comes around. Hindus feel no compassion for those living in horrible poverty and need, because they believe they are receiving payback for the evil deeds they committed in their past life. If you help the poor, they feel, you may be stopping them from achieving the penance they need to move on to a better place in their next life.

They do not have proper respect for women. And you may take your pick as to whom to worship, as there are many Gods to choose from. Which one will you choose to serve? And what will happen to you if you choose the wrong one?

HOW CAN A MAN KNOW THE WAY TO GO?

The true God has made it very easy for us to find our way to paradise. We must simply acknowledge the truth that we are all sinners in need of God's plan for salvation, which is to accept his Son, Jesus Christ, as our Lord and Savior. If you think you can analyze these false religions and develop a plan to get to heaven, or you simply want to risk your eternity by betting that you will not need a savior because you will never sin, that is your prerogative. The bottom line is that God is in control, and He has provided the only way we can get to heaven. Most religions believe in a heaven and a hell. So, the key is to ask yourself "What is my plan for getting to heaven and staying away from hell?"

I cannot understand why any individual with questions about the afterlife, would not take the time to research every religion. The most important thing is to understand where you are headed after you die.

We began this chapter by examining the religion of the ancient Egyptians. Now I want to take a quick look at how that religion and its disciples prepare for their afterlife:

The Egyptians believed their bodies would continue to exist after death. Their daily life pursuits would continue the same. Their number one concern was that there was no guarantee of getting to heaven. To get there, they would have to undertake a fierce underworld journey, capped off with a face-to-face final judgement, before they were able to enter. Several important preparations were required to achieve their goal:

1) **Funerary Items** must be purchased from temple for protection, guidance, etc.

2) **Other Essentials** must also be purchased -- food, clothing and shabtis (small funerary statuettes) and the Book of the Dead. This is not a book as we know it, but a collection of images and spells. Shabtis were small statuettes inscribed with a spell. It was thought that these statues would come to life once their owner had reached paradise. Then they would perform all the physical duties that were require.

3) **A coffin was also needed** and it must be covered by spells and prayers.

4) **Tombs must be built:** (called houses of eternity). Ancient Egyptians believed Tombs had the power to restore life.

Egyptians believed in a heaven and a hell. They sought to protect themselves in the afterlife by clothing their bodies with amulets and jewelry. They believed the jewels contained magical powers that would keep them from harm, (like occult practices of today). For example, heart-scarabs were placed over the dead person's heart to keep it from being separated from the body in the underworld.

The bottom line here is that you have an ancient civilization believing in good and evil; heaven and hell. They understood this from Adam and Eve. The serpent knew the free will gift given to man could not protect him from the demonic realm. Man wants the instant gratification that sin brings. Contrary to God's wishes, man abandons his dependence on God to pursue his own pleasures and desires. Yet God says again and again that we are to **"Trust Him in all things"** (Proverbs 3:5.) Trust is the foundation of our Faith.

They were devout followers of the sun god Inti, but they worshiped many other gods as well, including their ancestors, and offered burnt offerings to obtain their blessing.

Next up, we have the ancient Greeks. Their gods were involved in all aspects of human life--work, politics, marriage, theater, etc. The gods of the pantheon were very human-like as well, meaning they had flaws like jealousy, greed, vanity, and anger.

As far as the Greeks were concerned, death was merely the absence of consciousness and it was not to be feared. Socrates said, "To fear death is nothing more than to think oneself wise, when one is not." They had no concept of heaven or hell. They believed that the soul left the body at death, like a puff of wind, but that it continued in some other form. Interestingly, those who did good in life were not rewarded, and those who were evil were not punished. The spirit then went on a journey to a place called the underworld (Hades).

We have reviewed ancient civilizations who have gods and believe in an afterlife. We have also reviewed ancient civilizations that believed in many gods but do not have a plan for their afterlife.

Lastly, we have reviewed the atheists, who do not believe in God or life after death. The only thing that remains at the end of an atheist's life is the anxiety of or fear of death (thanatophobia).

Jesus shed His divine nature to clothe Himself in humanity. He has triumphed over Satan through His death, burial, and res-urrection, and is now legally able to take back control of the earth. The Bible is clear that the devil is in charge of the earth. Jesus acknowledged this fact when he said, **"I WILL NO LONGER TALK MUCH WITH YOU, FOR <u>THE RULER OF THIS WORLD IS COMING, AND HE HAS NOTHING IN ME</u>." (JOHN 14:30, NKJV)**

The devil and his demons work in the minds of humankind. Think of it as being similar to your TV. The signals from broad-cast transmitters are in the air and your TV picks up these signals and allows you to see and hear this broadcast. As the Bible says in Ephesians 2:1-3, **"AND YOU WERE DEAD IN YOUR OFFENSES AND SINS, IN WHICH YOU PREVIOUSLY WALKED ACCORDING TO THE COURSE OF THIS WORLD, ACCORDING TO THE PRINCE OF THE POWER OF THE AIR, OF THE SPIRIT THAT IS NOW WORKING IN THE SONS OF DISOBEDIENCE. AMONG THEM WE TOO ALL PREVIOUSLY LIVED IN THE LUSTS OF OUR FLESH, INDULGING THE DESIRES OF THE FLESH AND OF THE MIND, AND WERE BY NATURE CHILDREN OF WRATH, JUST AS THE REST..."**

At some time in the past, Satan gathered up one-third of the angels and involved them in a futile attempt to overthrow God Himself and take control of His throne. They were defeated and God cast them down to earth. The devil failed but remained in the office God gave him. His spirit of selfishness and pure evil was passed down to humans. For God to regain earth and humankind, He had to give of Himself. This is in fact why Satan is called "the god of this age." Jesus did not deserve to die, yet He took our place (1 Peter 3:18). This is what is called "substitutionary atonement." Jesus had not sinned, so His death paid our legal debt in full.

HUMANKIND'S TWO MAJOR ISSUES:

1) Humans were born, not evolved from a primate. You were born with a free will and your choices determine where you are headed. Animals do not have free will. They rely on instinct. This is why birds build nests in trees, or fly south for the winter, and why bears dig holes in which to hibernate, etc.

2) There is a heaven and a hell and it is your choice that determines where you are headed. Reviewing the ancient civilizations, we determined that each has a path to either heaven or hell. If you were to look up a definition for sin you would find that sin is regarded in Judaism and Christianity as the deliberate and

purposeful violation of the will of God. In its most basic form, it simply means 'to miss the mark'!

What is God's way back to Him? He wants to Trust in what He has done for us, which is sending His Son to suffer and die in our behalf. Keep in mind that it is all God's doing, and we cannot help Him. We simply must accept what He has done. In the Garden of Eden, Adam had a choice: to obey God's command or to take a bite of the forbidden fruit.

But one may say nothing can happen without God's permission. The Bible asks, **"WHO IS THERE WHO SPEAKS AND IT COMES TO PASS, UNLESS THE LORD HAS COMMANDED IT?" (LAMENTATIONS 3:37)** The Good News Translation reads **"THE WILL OF THE LORD IS ALWAYS CARRIED OUT."** So why would God allow Adam and Eve to eat the forbidden fruit?

Before tackling this most difficult issue of, "If nothing happens without God's approval, how did sin get into our world?" Let's review some of what we know about God. The only limitations He possesses are those He creates Himself. An example would be the old question, Can God create a rock so heavy that He cannot lift? My friend Hank Hanegraaff, in his book 'The Complete Bible Answer Book, writes, "This question is a classic straw man that has most Christians looking like the proverbial deer in the headlights. At best, it challenges God's omnipotence. At worst, it undermines His existence."[3]

God cannot do all things. For example, He cannot lie (Hebrews 6:18), He cannot be tempted (James 1:13), He cannot die (Psalm 102:25-27). Hank further clarified this by saying that it is impossible to make a one-sided triangle! Therefore, it is impossible to make a rock too heavy to be moved. So, the bottom line is God can do anything consistent with His nature. If something is logically possible, He can do it.

---

[3] Hannegraaff, Hank, "The Complete Bible Answer Book," (Thomas Nelson: Nashville) 2016

GOD IS ALL-POWERFUL

<u>God is Omnipotent.</u> *He has unlimited power. Genesis 1:1 says,* **"In the beginning God created the heavens and the earth."** *And Jeremiah 32:1 (ESV} says,* **"Ah, Lord God! It is You who have made the heavens and the earth by your great power and by your outstretched arm! Nothing is too hard for you."**

<u>God is Omnipresent.</u> *He is everywhere at the same time.* **Jeremiah 23:23-24 says, "Can a man hide himself in hiding places so I do not see him?" Declares the Lord. "Do I not fill the heavens and the earth?" Declares the Lord.** *And Deuteronomy 4:39 (ESV) adds,* **"Know therefore today, and lay it to your heart, that the Lord is God in heaven above and on the earth beneath: there is no other."**

<u>God is Omniscient.</u> *He knows everything! 1 John 3:20 (b) says,* **"...for God is greater than our heart <u>and knows all things</u>." And Psalm 139:4 (ESV) tells us, "Even before a word is on my tongue, behold, O Lord, You know it all together."**

CHAPTER THREE

HOW DID THINGS GO SO WRONG?

**"YOU WERE THE ANOINTED CHERUB
WHO COVERS,
AND I PLACED YOU THERE.
YOU WERE ON THE HOLY MOUNTAIN OF GOD;
YOU WALKED IN THE MIDST OF
THE STONES OF FIRE.
YOU WERE BLAMELESS IN YOUR WAYS
FROM THE DAY YOU WERE CREATED
UNTIL UNRIGHTEOUSNESS WAS FOUND IN YOU.
BY THE ABUNDANCE OF YOUR TRADE
YOU WERE INTERNALLY FILLED WITH VIOLENCE,
AND YOU SINNED;
THEREFORE I HAVE CAST YOU AS PROFANE
FROM THE MOUNTAIN OF GOD."
(EZEKIEL 28:14-16)**

Before the earth was formed, before 'Time' was a reality, God created angels (Psalm 104:4). The highest of these was Lucifer, which means light bearer or shining one. He was a magnificent being, full of wisdom and perfect in beauty. He was the anointed Cherub who walked and talked to God in the garden of Eden. Then one day something terrible happened.

Lucifer became Satan.

Ezekiel explains in chapter 28 of the book that bears his name. The bottom line is that Lucifer was overcome by pride. He said, "I will ascend above the heights of the clouds. I will be like the most-High."

Lucifer is now the enemy of God. His goal is to usurp God's authority and occupy His throne.

How could Lucifer do such a thing? It was possible only because our God does not create robots. He created Lucifer the same way He created man; with a free will.

Lucifer thought he was smarter and stronger than God, and had many of the created angels thinking the same way and ready to back his coup attempt. It is beyond reason to imagine how they thought they could succeed.

GOD KNOWS EVERYTHING BEFORE IT HAPPENS

Deuteronomy 29:29) tells us that, **"THE SECRET THINGS BELONG TO THE LORD OUR GOD. . ."** Perhaps the devil thought he could pull this off, forgetting that God can read our thoughts before the chemicals come together in our brains to produce those thoughts. Nothing catches him by surprise. Surely God knew that Lucifer would rebel before He even created him. He was aware of the evil he would bring -- the wars, diseases, the tragedies of all kinds. He knew how Lucifer would twist and misuse God's great gifts – like sex -- bringing about the perversions that threaten to tear our society apart.

I personally think it's disgusting that we now set aside an entire month to "honor" the gay community, while the men who fought and died to keep us free get only one day.

In an article by Josh Davis, staff evangelist for the Prophetic Observer, he spells out how far our country has fallen.[4] The month of June is celebrated as pride month. Major corporations have caved in to

---

4 'The Pride Charade," by Josh Davis, The Prophetic Observer, August, 2023

meet the demands of an estimated 7.2 percent (gays) of the entire population of the United States. According to a recent Gallup poll, some of those corporations have lost billions of dollars from supporting the gay agenda. Bud Light, after partnering with transgender activist Dylan Mulvaney, has lost $15 billion in revenue. Target is another retailer who hitched its star to selling and promoting pride merchandise, even to the point of introducing gay products and gay books to children. They also introduced products from Abprallen brand. One sweater said, "Cure transphobia not trans people." This brand also has products that praise the demonic world. One such item is an enamel pin that includes the satanic goat-headed idol Baphomet with the inscription 'Satan respects pronouns.' Target was estimated to have lost $10 to $15 billion in 10 days!

Target is not alone, there are also Kohl's, North Face, even Chick-fil-A. In 2012, the latter organization stopped supporting many Christian organizations, including the Fellowship of Christian Athletes, and the Salvation Army. How could such a thing occur, especially given that the founder of Chick-fil-A, Truett Cathy, had very strong religious convictions. The company's official statement read "The company exists to glorify God by being a faithful steward of all that is entrusted to us." Mr. Cathy was a godly man, so I doubt very much that he would approve some of the recent decisions the current company leaders have made. The decision to stop supporting the Salvation Army and Fellowship of Christian Athletes came five years after Mr. Cathy's passing, and after pressure from the LGBTQ+ community.

As a business owner, I certainly sympathize with Mr. Cathy. I completely understand the mechanics of such a decision. No matter what I want for my company, at the end of the day, whoever is CEO after I'm gone can do whatever he or she wants, even if it completely invalidates my previous wishes. Welcome to corporate America.

There is tremendous pressure for all companies to give in to pressure from the gay community, and that includes professional sports teams. Consider the Los Angeles Dodgers. For their 10th annual 'Pride Night at Dodger Stadium' the Dodgers invited the 'Sisters of perpetual Indulgence' to attend as honored guests. These "sisters" are drag queens who dress as nuns. Their motto is "Go forth and sin some more." An outpouring of negative responses from the Dodgers' Catholic fans was swift and resulted in the Dodgers uninviting the sisters. This, in turn, increased the pressure applied by the LGBTQ+ community to restore the invitation, and the Dodger organization folded like a cheap suit.

At the end of the day, we are in a war, not with the LGBTQ+ community, but with Satan and his demons. **"FOR OUR STRUGGLE IS NOT AGAINST FLESH AND BLOOD, BUT AGAINST THE RULERS, AGAINST THE POWERS, AGAINST THE WORLD FORCES OF THIS DARKNESS, AGAINST THE SPIRITUAL FORCES OF WICKEDNESS IN THE HEAVENLY PLACES" (EPHESIANS 6:12).**

Josh Davis concluded his thoughts by stating that one of Satan's greatest tools was to get people (especially in the USA) to worship themselves instead of God. The truth is that we cannot know ourselves until we first know God.

Tragically, we live in a world and a society that has moved very far away from God. Take a long hard look at what's going on in the world around you and tell me what you see: Deranged people attacking and killing grammar school children. People being beaten and killed because of the color of their skin or their ethnic background. Killings in prayer groups. Wars based on greed. When will it stop? Unfortunately, we know from what the Bible teaches that these various acts of violence will get worse and worse.

But if you think that all this evil has come from God, then I would like to sell you the Delaware Memorial Bridge. If you were to ask the man or woman on the street, I would bet that they are all interested in getting back to the America of the fifties and sixties, but are unwilling to do what is necessary to achieve that goal. My prayer is that the Lord will open the eyes of the spiritually blind, who have believed the lies of Satan.

I know that it can be discouraging to see that evil seems to be winning here in the 21st century. But be assured, a day of judgment is coming. Satan's final "reward" will come when he is cast into the lake of fire that will burn for all eternity. Here is the Irony of it all; Those individuals who sin and worship Satan they will all meet in hell, where they will suffer God's wrath for all eternity.

CHAPTER FOUR

SIGNS THAT JESUS IS COMING SOON!

> *"NOW LEARN THE PARABLE FROM THE FIG TREE: AS SOON AS ITS BRANCH HAS BECOME TENDER AND SPROUTS ITS LEAVES, YOU KNOW THAT SUMMER IS NEAR; SO YOU TOO, WHEN YOU SEE ALL THESE THINGS, RECOGNIZE THAT HE IS NEAR, RIGHT AT THE DOOR. (MATTHEW 24:32-33)*

As every tick of the clock continues to bring us closer to the end of the age, and America continues to be less Christian, look for divine judgment to fall on our nation. As Galatians 6:7 says, **"DO NOT BE DECEIVED; GOD WILL NOT BE MOCKED, FOR YOU REAP WHATEVER YOU SOW."**

If you sow to the flesh, and are led by your own selfish desires, the only thing the flesh can produce is corruption.

In this chapter, I want to talk about some of the important signs of Christ's coming. Of course, knowing that His return is just around the corner should not make any difference in the way we live. As Jesus Himself said, **"THEREFORE BE ON THE ALERT, FOR YOU DO NOT KNOW WHICH DAY YOUR LORD IS COMING. BUT BE SURE OF THIS, THAT IF THE HEAD OF THE HOUSE HAD KNOWN AT WHAT TIME OF THE NIGHT THE THIEF WAS COMING, HE WOULD HAVE BEEN ON THE ALERT AND WOULD NOT HAVE ALLOWED HIS**

HOUSE TO BE BROKEN INTO. FOR THIS REASON YOU MUST BE READY AS WELL; FOR THE SON OF MAN IS COMING AT AN HOUR WHEN YOU DO NOT THINK HE WILL" (MATTHEW 24:42-44).

But on the other hand, if we know that His return is imminent, then we should have abundant energy and drive to carry out the business that He has entrusted to us, His followers.

FIRST AND FOREMOST, KEEP YOUR EYES ON ISRAEL. IT IS GOD'S STOPWATCH FOR THE END!

Who wants Israel eliminated? Foremost in this crowd is all the Muslim nations, plus the radical terrorist factions they harbor. The word they use most often is "Jihad," which means "struggle." They have dedicated themselves to the destruction of Israel by any means possible. They have been defeated again and again in their efforts to drive Israel into the sea, but refuse to give up. Their unreasoning hatred for Israel and the Jewish people has brought untold misery and destruction on their own people, but they refuse to work for peace.

Their end game is to bring about a new global caliphate. They desire to install Sharia law (a government ruled by the clergy using commentaries on the Qur'an). The Muslim world will stop at nothing to win over our young people. Their use of the internet is remarkable, entrapping and manipulating young minds to believe the lie.

Believe it or not, the Jewish/Arab conflict dates back to Abraham and his descendants, starting with a boyhood argument between two brother – Ishmael, the father of the Arab nations, and Isaac, the father of the Jews. This conflict would seriously elevate in 1948 when Israel became a nation, touching off fury throughout the Islamic world.

Since then, Israel has endured suicide bombers, missile attacks, terrorist killings and many political threats from all nations. In 2014, Israel was bombed for 50 days straight by the Palestinians, with over 4,000 rockets fired from Gaza. Also in 2014, Iran proposed and sanctioned the richest terror group, Isis. This group seized radioactive material in Iraq. Their ultimate desire is to raise a Black Flag over the White House.

THE SIGN OF LIVING FOR PLEASURE

Another sign of Christ's return is given in Luke 17:28-30: **"IT WAS THE SAME AS HAPPENED IN THE DAYS OF LOT: THEY WERE EATING, THEY WERE DRINKING, THEY WERE BUYING, THEY WERE SELLING, THEY WERE PLANNING, THEY WERE BUILDING; BUT ON THE DAY THAT LOT WENT OUT FROM SODOM IT RAINED FIRE AND BRIMSTONE FROM HEAVEN AND DESTROYED THEM ALL. <u>IT WILL BE JUST THE SAME ON THE DAY THAT THE SON OF MAN IS REVEALED.</u>"** (Emphasis mine.)

In the days of Abraham's nephew Lot (about 4,000 years ago,) people were not reading their scriptures, nor did they have an interest in the things of God. In other words, they were an awful lot like those of us living in the 2024. Men and women were eating and drinking and having a good time. This is what they lived for! Today, as in the days of lot, gluttony and drunken parties were a way of life. Lot was a wealthy man who had much livestock, many servants and all the "good things" life has to offer. But he chose to close his eyes to the wickedness of his ungodly neighbors.

THE SIGN OF HOMOSEXUALITY

Homosexuality was rampant in those days, much like now, and people did not care about it. Their attitude was live and let live, no matter what God had to say. People today really do not care that sin is raging all around them. Most of them are not interested in anything spiritual. They are not aware that rampant homosexuality is another sign that the end is near. In the time of Lot, destruction came in the firm of fire and brimstone rained down from heaven on Sodom and Gomorrah. This time, it will come in the return of Christ to the world He created.

Today, we are all taught that we must be tolerant. We must accept it when others mock God. This group of evil doers continues to increase. They have even reached the highest levels in our government. The irony is that they are oblivious to the calamitous events that will befall them.

I have already mentioned that the people of Lot's Day accepted homosexuality as normal. For that to happen, the children of that day had to grow up believing that homosexual behavior was normal. Parents and educators were responsible for the furtherance of this sin. This was accepted, and not only in Sodom and Gomorrah. The Bible says, **"JUST AS SODOM AND GOMORRAH AND THE SURROUNDING CITIES WHICH LIKEWISE INDULGED IN SEXUAL IMMORALITY AND PURSUED UNNATURAL DESIRE, SERVE AS AN EXAMPLE BY UNDERGOING A PUNISHMENT OF ETERNAL FIRE." (JUDE 1:7)**

Today, homosexuality is regarded as an "orientation" like being left-handed. Changes that are taking place in attitudes worldwide. This new "tolerant" attitude came over time, beginning with the decriminalization of homosexual acts. Suddenly, homosexuality was no long regarded as a perversion, but as an acceptable lifestyle practiced by a minority of men and women in our society. Their major push in recent years has been to bring about international acceptance of gay marriage. Now, on top of this, the gay movement is promoting acceptance of transgender issues. Children are being encouraged to change their sexual identity. If you were born as a boy, but think you would be happier as a girl, go ahead and change your gender. Parents are even encouraging their children to change. Thus, momentary confusion or frustration may result in a horrible mistake that cannot be undone.

Many children today have no time for any belief system. Christianity is laughed at by those who have a "woke" attitude. What is happening is that children today are calling evil good, and good evil (Isaiah 5:21).

Listen up! God will not be mocked. He says, **"DO NOT BE DECEIVED, YOU REAP WHATEVER YOU SOW" (GALATIANS 6:7)**. Do not believe every spirit. Homosexuality is contrary to God's natural order. In Corinthians 6:9-10, the Bible lists this sin as one that will prevent you from entering heaven. It is critical to understand that God loves you and if you repent of this sin He will forgive you, and entrance to heaven is available.

And yet, even though this is true, the spread of the acceptance of homosexuality is not a good thing for our world. In fact, it is a sure sign that the end days are upon us.

THE SIGN OF ANTISEMITISM

Widespread antisemitism is another sign of Jesus imminent return. Fundamentally, antisemitism is hatred for the Jews, and it has been going on for centuries. Hitler wasn't the first to try destroy the Jewish people and, sadly, he will not be the last. As I write these words, war is once again raging in the Middle East, after the Palestinian terrorist group, Hamas, launched a surprise attack on Israel. Hundreds of Israelis, most of them civilians, died in the attack. But now, Hamas is paying the price, as Israel has responded with a full-scale attack on Gaza, which is Hamas' home base. In the United States and around the world, there have been many protests and demonstrations denouncing the Jews for their assault on Gaza. There has been no mention that Hamas started it all by launching a surprise attack on innocent Jewish civilians, killing many families, including moms, dads and young children. In the aftermath of Hamas' attack on Israel, it was reported that many Jewish newborns were beheaded by the invaders. Such viciousness and hatred are hard to fathom. Why, then, are the Israelis being criticized for defending themselves> This is yet another sign of worldwide anti-Semitism.

The Bible makes it clear that prior to the Lord's return, Israel and its people, will be hated as never before--and I believe we are seeing the start of that right now. Why is that? The website, "Got Questions' offers six possible reasons:

1) Racial Theory: Jews are hated because they are considered to be an inferior race.

2) Economic Theory: They are hated because they possess enormous wealth.

3) Outsiders Theory: They are different.

4) Scapegoat Theory: They are considered to be the root cause for the world's problems.

5) Deicide Theory: They are blamed for killing Jesus.

6) Chosen people: They are hated because they arrogantly state that they are the chosen ones of God.

To be completely honest with you, none of these reasons make much sense to me. People who hate the Jews may try to use these "reasons" to justify their behavior. But I believe that the real reason the world hates the Jews is that it also hates Jesus Christ, the King of the Jews.

Couple this with the fact that after 2,000 years without a homeland, the Jews were given back their country in 1948. This hatred of Christ is world renowned.

And what about the charge that Jews arrogantly proclaim that they are God's chosen people? The fact is they are, indeed God's Chosen people, a fact the Bible tells us about again and again. (See, Deuteronomy 14:2, for example.)

The Jews were chosen by God to bring forth His word (Jesus) to redeem the world from sin and eventually cast Satan and his demons into the lake of fire. And despite the efforts of the Babylonians, Persians, Assyrians, Egyptians, Hittites and Nazis, the Jewish people are still thriving!

The truth is that Israel will never be eradicated. We know this because Romans 11:26 tells us that someday all Israel will be saved. God must preserve nation of Israel and its people until His plans for them are fulfilled.

OTHER PRESENT-DAY SIGNS:

Other Signs of Jesus' return include:

A worldwide abandonment of religious beliefs.

The Gospel will be restored (Daniel 2:44, Acts 3: 19-21).

Many Jews will be brought home to Israel from the countries to which they have been scattered. (Jeremiah 16:14-16).

Evil and Wickedness will run wild (2 Timothy 3:1, Matthew 24:37.)

Jesus assures us that He is returning to earth, (Matthew 24:36-37) and then adds, "But of that day and hour no one knows, not even the angels of heaven, nor the Son, but the Father alone."

CHAPTER FIVE

AS IT WAS IN THE DAYS OF NOAH

Jesus said that just before He returns to earth, the world will be very much like it was in the time of Moses. Take a good look around you, and you will see how these words are coming true.

As was true in Noah's day, Spiritual Decline is all around us and society is becoming increasingly corrupt.

And there are many other similarities.

Population was and is expanding (See Genesis 6)

Violence is rampant upon the earth. Genesis 6:12 says, **"GOD LOOKED ON THE EARTH, AND BEHOLD, IT WAS CORRUPT; FOR ALL FLESH HAD CORRUPTED THEIR WAY UPON THE EARTH."**

If you want to see the similarities between then and now, just take a read through your local newspaper.

In Lot's lifetime, people were eating, drinking, marrying, and doing other everyday things until it was time to enter the ark. They had no idea at all regarding what was about to happen to them until the rain began to fall. And not just rain, but torrential rain. Up to this point, people were accustomed to the earth's watering via a heavy mist that rose up from the ground. In other words, they had never experienced rain, much less hard rain, prior to the flood.

At this point people were confused, but not necessarily afraid. The Bible says, **"IT WAS THE SAME AS HAPPENED IN THE DAYS OF LOT: THEY WERE EATING, THEY WERE DRINKING, THEY WERE BUYING, THEY WERE SELLING, THEY WERE PLANTING, THEY WERE BUILDING; BUT ON THE DAY THAT LOT WENT OUT FROM SODOM IT RAINED FIRE AND BRIMSTONE FROM HEAVEN AND DESTROYED THEM ALL" (LUKE 17:28-30).**

Jude 1:7 tells us that the people who lived in Sodom & Gomorrah had given themselves over to 'fornication' and going after 'strange flesh.' Speaking of strange flesh, 23 countries have now sanctioned same sex marriage. God condemns this behavior, but man now sees it as natural. We see from Jude that sexual immorality and homosexuality had taken control of all the people in Sodom, and everything that men thought about was evil. Most people who engage in homosexual behavior really and truly think that what they are doing is 'normal.' Over time, people stopped thinking it was a crime, only a sickness. This then led to abandonment of traditional values. Ancients viewed this as simply another lifestyle.

How does this compare with 2023? Our world today is full of terrorists, overrun with violence, drugs and many other types of evil, and now our children are being told they can choose their gender. Transgender activists are basically saying, "God, you made a mistake when you made me." Some who have changed their gender include Bruce Jenner (Caitlyn Jenner), Zaya Wade (daughter of Dwayne

Wade), Chaz Bono (daughter of Sonny & Cher), Nats Getty, (related to Sir John Paul Getty of the Getty Oil Family) Renee Richards, just to name a few.

After Noah entered the ark, the flood came and killed everything that was alive. Only eight people survived. Similarly, the return of Jesus will be quicker than the blink of an eye. Noah's neighbors had seen him working on the ark, and laughed at him for building a boat so far from the ocean. Undoubtedly, they had seen him going in and out of the big ship as he and his sons worked on it. They saw this so often, in fact, that they didn't think anything about it.

Then one day, he went inside, the door was shut for the last time, and rain began to pour down. God literally opened the great fountains of the deep, followed by the 'windows of heaven,' a biblical source of water. Once this began to happen, there was no hope for those who remained outside the ark. Imagine their panic and despair when they realized they had missed their only chance to be spared.

Think about this. No human being had never seen a rainbow because it had never rained. Plants and flowers had been watered by an early-morning mist, similar to dew. The world had never seen so much as a gentle rain before, much less a catastrophic flood.

Before Jesus returns, this world will once again experience something that no man or woman has ever seen previously. Before our Lord establishes His church, he will come for those who are living the Christian life. This is called "The Rapture." The dead in Christ will rise first. After that, the faithful who are still living for God will also rise into the sky. As these godly people ascend, they will all be clothed in spiritual bodies. In 1 Corinthians 15:50-58, the apostle Paul writes that, **"mortal bodies must put on immortality in order to enter heaven..."** He adds that those who are still living at that time will not experience death, but will be transformed in "the twinkling of an eye."

This rapture event signals a period characterized by hell on earth for those who do not belong to Jesus, "A time of Jacob's trouble." The

Bible makes it clear that those who believe in Christ are the salt and light that seasons and preserves the earth. One can only imagine how difficult it will be here after all the salt and light has been removed from the world.

Oh, how deep and dark the wickedness will be. Yes, many will turn to Christ during this time, but they will suffer through years of persecution and tribulation.

I am certain that Noah preached to the crowds that were watching as he and his sons built a huge ship in the desert. He cried out to them to repent, warning them that judgment was near – but they would not listen. We also know that Lot was burdened with the evil and sexual perversions of his day (2 Peter 2:7). But as with Noah, his preaching fell on deaf ears. A we look around us, we can see that things are not much different here in the 21st century.

We are surrounded by violence and sexual perversion, and I am sure that God is running out of patience.

MAKE NO MISTAKE THESE ARE THE LAST DAYS. TURN AWAY FROM SIN BEFORE ITS TOO LATE.

The Lord knows that some will respond to my words by telling me that I'm crazy. But I'll respond to this by quoting 2 Peter 3:3-4. **"KNOWING THIS FIRST, THAT THERE SHALL COME IN SCOFFERS WALKING AFTER THEIR OWN LUSTS, AND SAYING, WHERE IS THE PROMISE OF HIS COMING? FOR SINCE THE FATHERS FELL ASLEEP, ALL THINGS CONTINUE AS THEY WERE FROM THE BEGINNING OF THE CREATION."**

Scoffers rely on their belief in the lie! They do not believe that Jesus will ever return to this earth. They trust in the belief of His returning. Not in the reality of His return. These same people have forgotten all of God's promises regarding salvation. They are aware of the judgment that is approaching, but they think it is a long way off--perhaps hundreds or even thousands of years. They are in for a terrible surprise.

Please remember that God does not want anyone to perish, but His patience has its limits. Scoffers presume upon the mercy and long-suffering of God, but they are seeing only what they want to see. They read the Bible and learn about God's judgments, but say, "Oh, that was the Old Testament God. He is now a kind and loving God who wouldn't pass judgment on anyone."

This is a complete misperception of who God is. The Bibe tells us that Jesus Christ is the same yesterday, today and forever (Hebrews 13:8). He does not change. The fifth chapter of Acts tells the story of a couple named Ananias and Saphira, who sold a piece of property and gave a portion of their profits to the church. That is a good thing, of course, and they would have been commended for their generosity. The problem was that they said they were giving everything they had earned to the church. This was not true, and God struck both dead because they had lied to the Holy Spirit. Again, God is merciful, but a day of judgment is coming like a thief in the night.

The Bible tells us in 2 Peter 3:8, **"BUT DO NOT FORGET THIS ONE THING, DEAR FRIENDS: WITH THE LORD A DAY IS LIKE 1,000 YEARS. . . HE IS PATIENT WITH YOU, NOT WANTING ANYONE TO PERISH, BUT EVERYONE TO COME TO REPENTANCE."** You see in God's eyes all things are equally near and present to Him. For those who scoff at the idea that Christ will return, simply look at the days of Noah. Do you think Noah had any scoffers? Indeed, he did. Just think how ridiculous he looked to his neighbors? Here is a guy building an enormous ship in the middle of a desert. A scoffer is anyone who laughs or ridicules another person for their beliefs. The Bible says, **"HE WHO CORRECTS A SCOFFER GETS DISHONOR FOR HIMSELF, AND HE WHO REPROVES A WICKED MAN GETS INSULTS FOR HIMSELF" (PROVERBS 9:7-8).** Fools are quick to speak because they consider themselves wise, when in fact they are fools, not knowing right from wrong, quick to anger and very arrogant about their own opinions!

If you read your Bible, you have probably tried to find mention of the United States in the last days. Where will we be? Whose side will we be on in the final battle of Armageddon? Will God use us to usher in His kingdom? Consider Daniel chapter 7, which mentions four beasts (a lion, bear, eagle, and leopard). Fast forward to Revelation 13, where the Apostle John sees a vision of one beast. This beast has the body of a leopard, the feet of a bear, mouth of a Lion and the ten horns of the ten-horned beast. (This beast represents the new world order, or the revived Roman Empire, and the eagle is no longer mentioned.) Could it be that the eagle (USA) opposed this new order and was no longer a world power? Or, since over 40 percent of the U.S. population is Christian, it could be that when the rapture comes, it will vastly reduce our population and leave the U.S. with major internal problems.

CHAPTER SIX

WHY DOES GOD ALLOW DISEASES AND ALL TYPES OF EVIL?

Make no mistake. God is good and does not want man to suffer. We suffer because sin is in the world. Author C.S. Lewis wrote in his book, *Mere Christianity:*

"My argument against God was that the universe seemed so cruel and unjust. But how had I got the idea of just and unjust? A man does not call a line crooked unless he has some idea of a straight line. What was I comparing this universe with when I called it unjust?" Lewis concluded, "If I find in myself a desire which no experience in this world can satisfy, the most probable explanation is that I was made for another world." [5]

Suffering was not in the world God designed for man. It came into the world due to man's rebellion against God.

It went like this: God gave man the earth, but man turned right around and very legally gave it to Satan as a consequence of sin. At that point, God could have squashed both man and Satan. Instead, acting legally, He sent His Son to redeem the earth. Man broke his relationship with God the minute Adam bit the fruit handed to him by Eve. It was at this time that Adam and Eve left the protection of God and the Garden where they enjoyed eternal life. Instead, they chose suffering and death.

Life on this planet has been full of pain and sorrow since then. Yes, there are moments of great joy. The birth of a child, the marriage of a man and woman who truly love each other, the breathtaking beauty of an amazing sunset. Events like these give us glimpses of the way God meant the world to be. But we are also plagued by war, crime, sickness, and pain.

The good news is that even in the midst of all this, we can be joyful because we know that in the end God will make it right. The Book of Revelation speaks of a time when there will be no more suffering, no more death, and we get a new earth!

One important thing to remember about suffering is that Jesus suffered. He says, **"IF ANYONE WOULD COME AFTER ME, LET HIM DENY HIMSELF AND TAKE UP HIS CROSS AND FOLLOW ME. FOR WHOEVER WOULD SAVE HIS LIFE WILL LOSE IT, BUT WHOEVER LOSES HIS LIFE FOR MY SAKE WILL SAVE IT"** (LUKE 9:23-24).

---

[5] Lewis, C.S., "Mere Christianity," Signature Classic.(London, England: William Collin) 2012

Because Adam and Eve disobeyed God, humankind must deal with the consequences of sin. Someone might say, "I didn't sin. I didn't eat any of the forbidden fruit, so why do I have death always looking over my shoulder?" The answer is that all men were in Adam, therefore all men share in Adam's choice." You were in Adam--maybe a few thousand years later -- but you were in him! God knew this and because He loves His children, He provided a way for us to get back what was taken from us, and that way is the death, burial, and resurrection of His Son Jesus Christ. He paid the penalty for our sins and provided a way for us to return to the shelter of God's arms.

God made this amazing sacrifice because he cares deeply about the men and women He created. He is our Father, and He loves us the way a human parent loves his children, only many times stronger and deeper. As part of the human race, we have the distinct honor of loving Him and thanking Him for His Son. Think about a Holy God crowning man, as Psalm 8:5-6 says, ". . .and You crown Him with glory and majesty..." Sinners redeemed by the blood are now saints.

CHAPTER SEVEN:

HOW TO RECOGNIZE THE ANTICHRIST

THEN I SAW ANOTHER BEAST COMING UP OUT OF THE EARTH; AND HE HAD TWO HORNS LIKE A LAMB, AND HE SPOKE AS A DRAGON. HE PERFORMS GREAT SIGNS, SO THAT HE EVEN MAKES FIRE COME DOWN OUT OF THE SKY TO THE EARTH IN THE PRESENCE OF PEOPLE. AND HE CAUSES ALL, THE SMALL AND THE GREAT, THE RICH AND THE POOR, AND THE FREE AND THE SLAVES, TO BE GIVEN A MARK ON THEIR RIGHT HANDS OR ON THEIR FOREHEADS, AND HE DECREES THAT NO ONE WILL BE ABLE TO BUY OR TO SELL, EXCEPT THE ONE WHO HAS THE MARK, EITHER THE NAME OF THE BEAST OR THE NUMBER OF HIS NAME. HERE IS WISDOM. LET HIM WHO HAS UNDERSTANDING CALCULATE THE NUMBER OF THE BEAST, FOR THE NUMBER IS THAT OF A MAN; AND HIS NUMBER IS SIX HUNDRED AND SIXTY-SIX. (REVELATION 13:11,13, 16-18)

The Bible is clear that Satan is the ruler of this present-day earth. For example, take a moment to read Luke 4:5-7: **"AND HE LED HIM UP AND SHOWED HIM ALL THE KINGDOMS OF THE WORLD IN A MOMENT OF TIME AND THE DEVIL SAID TO HIM, 'I WILL GIVE YOU ALL THIS DOMAIN AND ITS GLORY; FOR IT HAS BEEN HANDED OVER TO ME, AND I GIVE IT TO WHOMEVER I WISH. THEREFORE, IF YOU WORSHIP BEFORE ME, IT SHALL BE YOURS."**

Jesus says in John 12:31, **"NOW JUDGEMENT IS UPON THIS WORLD, NOW THE RULER OF THIS WORLD WILL BE CAST OUT."**

Make no mistake, there is a spiritual battle going on behind the scenes. There are demons assigned to every nation, as well as to every state, province, or county in that nation. They are also assigned to every home, except those that are Christ-centered. The fact is that demons fear those who are filled with the Holy Spirit. The apostle John writes, **"YOU ARE OF GOD, MY LITTLE CHILDREN, AND HAVE OVERCOME THEM; BECAUSE GREATER IS HE THAT IS IN YOU THAN HE THAT IS IN THE WORLD." (1 JOHN 4:4)**

Recall Daniel's prayer, in chapter 10 of the book that bears his name. After he prayed, the angel Gabriel appeared and told him not to fear because his prayer had been answered three weeks ago.

According to the Bible, the message from God was impeded by the Prince of Persia—a demonic spirit, that ruled over the land. Only after the Archangel Michael interceded was Gabriel able to deliver his message. This is typical of the conflicts that are being waged all around us every day.

We all know instinctively that there is a spiritual world, and many of us are anxious to experience it, no matter what the consequences may be. It seems that more and more individuals are turning to horoscopes, tarot cards, and other forms of spiritism. Some visit psychics and mediums regularly. This is known as the occult. The occult requires a belief in the supernatural world. The word itself is derived from the Latin "occultus," which means secretive or hidden. Humankind's self-destructive tendencies now prevent us from looking up and acknowledging God. Our political leaders can offer no help whatsoever. They simply make our problems worse.

It seems like the leaders of countries all over this world are looking for war. Just last week president Biden set up a deal to sell weapons to Taiwan. China responded by stating that there will be a harsh reaction to this deal. China condemned Biden and sent fighter jets to patrol this region. Also, the Kremlin threatened use of nuclear weapons based on Ukraine using drones to attack Moscow. Russia reacted to the drone attacks by calling Ukraine a terrorist nation! Talk about the proverbial pot calling the kettle names. Satan surely laughs when he sees the hatred, division, and sorrow he and his demons have brought into this world. There is so much trouble all around us.

According to the United Nations, nearly 2.5 billion people do not have enough to eat right now. Millions are struggling for survival on the edge of starvation. Despite medical advances, the potential for diseases to spread, eventually escalating into a pandemic, are greater than ever before. The Centers for Disease Control says this increased risk is brought about by expanding air travel, increased human/animal contact, and lack of medical workers.

The CDC recently announced that an ancient medical issue has reared its ugly head in central Florida. Leprosy! [6]Long thought to be extinct in the United States, it is a devastating illness that eventually causes your tissues to degenerate to the point where your fingers and toes simply fall off. Today we call it Hansen's disease, or mycobacterium leprae, and in addition to the U.S., it can be found in India, Africa, and Latin America. You see, Satan is doing everything within his power to destroy us, whether by supernatural means or the revival of diseases that were once kept under control by modern medicine.

---

[6] Centers for Disease Control and Prevention, Case Report of Leprosy in Central Florida, USA, 2022 - Volume 29, Number 8—August 2023 - Emerging Infectious Diseases journal - CDC.

Another serious problem in developing countries is that diseases like leprosy drive the people--many of whom do not have access to simple medicines that could save their lives --directly into the hands of shamans and others who operate under the power of familiar spirits. People turn to familiar spirits because they want healing and answers to their problems. What they get, instead, are lies straight from the pit of hell. They may masquerade as angels, but they are not what they claim to be.

Many Bible verses warn us against engaging in any form of the occult. When you 'dabble' you open yourself up to demonic spirits. Many people think such behavior is harmless. Behind all these so-called truth-tellers stands the father of lies.

The Bible tells us to test the spirits to see whether they are from God or our ancient enemy, the devil. How do we do this? It's very simple. John writes, **"BELOVED, DO NOT BELIEVE EVERY SPIRIT, BUT TEST THE SPIRITS TO SEE WHETHER THEY ARE FROM GOD, BECAUSE MANY FALSE PROPHETS HAVE GONE OUT INTO THE WORLD. BY THIS YOU KNOW THE SPIRIT OF GOD: EVERY SPIRIT THAT CONFESSES THAT JESUS CHRIST HAS COME IN THE FLESH IS FROM GOD; AND EVERY SPIRIT THAT DOES NOT CONFESS JESUS IS NOT FROM GOD; THIS IS THE SPIRIT OF THE ANTICHRIST, OF WHICH YOU HAVE HEARD THAT IT IS COMING, AND NOW IT IS ALREADY IN THE WORLD." (1 JOHN 4:1-3)**

In his gospel, John quotes Jesus as telling the Pharisees, **"YOU ARE OF YOUR FATHER THE DEVIL, AND YOU WANT TO DO THE DESIRES OF YOUR FATHER. HE WAS A MURDERER FROM THE BEGINNING, AND DOES NOT STAND IN THE TRUTH BECAUSE THERE IS NO TRUTH IN HIM. WHENEVER HE SPEAKS A LIE, HE SPEAKS FROM HIS OWN NATURE, FOR HE IS A LIAR AND THE FATHER OF LIES." (JOHN 8:44)**

The occult has overtaken our American way of life. For many, God is like a box we keep on a shelf in our bedroom, labeled" use in case of emergency." God wants to be part of your life, every day every hour! And yet, as we near the time of our Lord's return, the darkness of occult deception will spread throughout the world--and then the anti-Christ will emerge onto the scene. Here are some ways to identify him, along with corresponding Bible verses, The Antichrist will:

A) **Emerge** from the restored Roman Empire (Daniel 7:7, Revelation 13:2)

B) **Rise** from obscurity...a little horn (Daniel 7:8)

C) **Speak** boastfully (Revelation 13:5)

D) **Blaspheme** God (Daniel 7:25)

E) **Oppress** the saints for 3-1/2 years (Revelation 13:7)

F) **Try to change** the law and calendar (Danie 7:25)

G) **Confirm** a covenant with the Jews (Daniel 9:27)

H) **Stop** the sacrifice & offerings in temple (Daniel 9:27, Matthew 24:15)

I) **Answer** to no man, but do what he pleases (Daniel 11:36)

J) **Show no interest in the religion of his ancestors (Daniel 11:37)**

K) **Not believe** in any god except for himself (Daniel 11:37)

L) **Have no regard** or dcsirc for women (Daniel 11:37)

M) **Claim** to be God (2 Thessalonian (2:4)

N) **Honor** a god of the military and conquer and divide the land (Daniels 11:39-44)

O) **Be preceded** by miracles, signs, and wonders (2 Thessalonians 2:9)

P) **Survive** a fatal injury (Revelation 13:3; 17:8)

Q) **Be empowered** by the devil (Revelation 13:2)

Dr. David Jeremiah's blog contains some additional information that will further help you recognize the Antichrist when he arrives on the scene:[7]

---

[7] See https://davidjeremiah.blog

First, many people will fall away from the faith. This apostasy began in ancient days (2 Timothy 4:10) and is accelerating today. After the rapture, the demonic world will no longer be restrained by the Holy Spirit. With the Holy Spirit being absent from the world, the apostasy will run rampant.

Secondly, the anti-Christ will arrive on the scene peaceably, but will seize the kingdom by intrigue (Daniel 11:21). He will start off as a lonely political figure, only to rise in the ranks and eventually take over. He will be handsome, intelligent and speak with great authority (Revelation 13:5-6), but much of what he says will be blasphemy. He will speak against the most-High and defy God as he starts his own religion.

Finally, the Lord says that after 42 months 'the deception of the devil is defeated.' Total and absolute defeat will occur at the battle of Armageddon. At this time, the Lord will arrive from heaven, riding a white horse. The battle will be over before it begins. Jesus will defeat the devil supernaturally, with the breath of His mouth (Daniel 8:25), and the false prophet and the Antichrist will be sent into the lake of fire (Revelation 19:20).

The most important question to ask is:

Where will you be when the Antichrist is unveiled?

If you are alive and living here on earth, you will be in a very bad spot. All your friends and family will most likely have been raptured or are dead. And yet, despite the desperation of the situation you find yourself in, there will be hope. The Bible is very clear that **"Whoever calls on the name of the Lord shall be saved"** (Romans 10:13).

Keep in mind that it's not a prayer that saves you, but rather the relationship you have with the living Christ. He saves you. Prayer is not the catalyst that activates salvation. <u>FAITH</u> in Christ is!

CHAPTER EIGHT

YOUR PAST HAS SHAPED YOUR FUTURE

". . . DO YOU NOT KNOW THAT THE UNRIGHTEOUS WILL NOT INHERIT THE KINGDOM OF GOD? DO NOT BE DECEIVED; NEITHER THE SEXUALLY IMMORAL, NOR IDOLATERS, NOR ADULTERERS, NOR HOMOSEXUALS, NOR THIEVES, NOR THE GREEDY, NOR THOSE HABITUALLY DRUNK, NOR VERBAL ABUSERS, NOR SWINDLERS, WILL INHERIT THE KINGDOM OF GOD. SUCH WERE SOME OF YOU; BUT YOU WERE WASHED, BUT YOU WERE SANCTIFIED, BUT YOU WERE JUSTIFIED IN THE NAME OF THE LORD JESUS CHRIST AND IN THE SPIRIT OF OUR GOD." (1 CORINTHIANS 6:9-11)

want to encourage you by sharing a bit of my own story.

Born and raised a Roman Catholic, I was educated at a Catholic grammar school, a Catholic high school, and a Jesuit university--Georgetown. I was a concrete catholic. In other words, I never asked any questions, but simply followed all the rules. One thing was evident, I loved the Lord! One day in prayer I asked Him to put me on the right road.

In those days I had many questions concerning Catholicism and my New American Standard Bible reinforced my thoughts. It seamed like a great divide in many areas. One example: The Lord said, "All have sinned and fallen short of the glory of God" (Romans 3:23-24). But the Catholic Church teaches that "Mary was conceived without sin."

I felt that if God wanted to exempt Mary, He would have said, "All have sinned, except Mary." In my book *Don't Miss the Celebration in Heaven,* I discuss another error in Catholic teaching, and that is the infallibility of the Pope.

Catholicism teaches that when the Pope speaks from St. Peter's chair (it is referred to as ex-cathedra) he is "infallible." The last such pronouncement was when Pope Pius XII stated that Mary was assumed to heaven. Wrong again! God says in Hebrews 9:27 that every human being is destined to die once, and to then go through the judgment. Only two people in all of history have gone directly to heaven without passing through judgment--Enoch and Elijah. The Old Testament tells us that Enoch walked with God and "God took him," and that Elijah was taken to heaven in a chariot of fire. One last point about Popes. Pope Eugene IV put Joan of Arc to death, while Benedict made her a saint! Which one do you believe? They can't both be right!

I could go on and on with issues connected to Catholic teachings, but you get the point. Undoubtedly, Mary, the mother of Jesus was a wonderful woman, full of grace and mercy. She was chosen to be the earthly mother of our Lord and Savior, and that has to the highest honor that any woman could ever receive. Jesus clearly loved her dearly, and was thinking about her even as he hung on the cross, telling his disciple, John, to take her into his home. (John 19:26)

But Jesus also made it clear that His mother was not to be worshiped. In the third chapter of Mark, we find this account:

"THEN HIS MOTHER AND HIS BROTHERS ARRIVED, AND STANDING OUTSIDE THEY SENT WORD TO

> **HIM AND CALLED HIM. A CROWD WAS SITTING AROUND HIM, AND THEY *SAID TO HIM, "BEHOLD, YOUR MOTHER AND YOUR BROTHERS ARE OUTSIDE LOOKING FOR YOU." ANSWERING THEM, HE SAID, "WHO ARE MY MOTHER AND MY BROTHERS?" LOOKING ABOUT AT THOSE WHO WERE SITTING AROUND HIM, HE *SAID, "BEHOLD MY MOTHER AND MY BROTHERS! FOR WHOEVER DOES THE WILL OF GOD, HE IS MY BROTHER AND SISTER AND MOTHER." (MARK 3:31-35)**

Clearly, the Roman Catholic adulation of Mary does not match with the New Testament accounts of her life. She was not and is not divine.

Have you spent part of your life believing erroneous doctrines? No problem. Thank God you can see those errors today and let them go. Thank Him for having you covered, and never forget where you came from.

For me, the transition from dark to light was easy, especially considering that I knew who Jesus was and what He did for mankind. My worst problem was that even though I knew about Jesus, I trusted in Mary and the church more than I trusted in Him. My faith was in works--in obeying the laws of the church and my lack of trust in Jesus would affect my eternity. One thing I must reiterate was my love for God, He knew my thoughts before the chemicals could come together in my head. He and He alone opened my eyes, and what a magnificent day it was for me when He did. Here is how it happened.

My wife would leave a 'spiritual book' on my nightstand every evening. Before daring to read it, I would check for the imprimatur (license by the Catholic Church signifying that a book is okay for Catholics to read}. You see, my wife went and got herself born again and for years she would leave something on the nightstand hoping I would read it. My rule was: No Imprimatur, no read! Until one day she left a book called *Born Again Catholic* by Albert Boudreau. There was an imprimatur so I read. Once I began reading, I could not put it down.

Check your past. What did your parents believe? What did they leave you with? Did they drag you to church with them? Note: Perfect church attendance, volunteer work, donations, visiting the poor, etc., will not get you into heaven. **God wants you to trust completely in his finished work on the cross!**

Frank Sinatra was once asked if he believed in God? His reply was, "I believe in nature, in the birds, the sea, the sky, in everything I can see or that there is real evidence for. If these things are what you meant by God, then I believe in God. But I don't believe in a personal God to whom I look for comfort or for a natural on the next roll of the dice."[8]

Consider these last words from Anton LaVey (founder of the American Satanic Church and author of the Satanic Bible). On his death bed, he reportedly said, "Oh my, oh my, what have I done? Something very wrong."[9] Obviously, what he saw influenced his words. He was terrified, realizing that he had been deceived by Satan and was now facing eternity in hell.

In Deuteronomy 30:19 the Lord told man to choose life. He said **"I HAVE SET BEFORE YOU LIFE AND DEATH, THE BLESSING AND THE CURSE. SO CHOOSE LIFE IN ORDER THAT YOU MAY LIVE, YOU AND YOUR DESCENDANTS."** In other words, do not chase after false religions and philosophies. Trust in God and in the love He showed when He sacrificed His Son in your stead!

Gods plan of salvation is simple. Believe in Jesus and trust in His Word. This is all you have to do. It is not difficult, although humans pile their man-made rules on top of it and try to make it seem harder than it really is. If you haven't accepted Christ's sacrificial death as

---

[8] "Frank Sinatra was spiritual not religious before it was cool," by Brandon Ambrosino, Vox.com, updated January 30, 2015

[9] See You Tube video by Rev. Alex Meadows, "Satanist Anton Lavey's Last Words"

payment for your transgressions, then you are still a sinner and in need of God's grace. You can ask Him right now, wherever you are, to save you and open the doors to Heaven so you can go in. At this very moment you can acknowledge in your heart that you are a sinner and in need of God's grace, and ask Him to save you for the kingdom of heaven. What you do not want is to spend eternity in Hell!

WHERE ARE YOU HEADED?

If you ask someone where he or she is going to go after they die, you will probably be told, "Heaven, I hope." Some will say, "I think I'm going to heaven!" while others may admit that they really don't have any idea what is going to happen, or they may tell you that they don't believe in an afterlife, and that death is the end of existence. All these answers can't possibly be right. So where does the truth lie?

You need to know God has a plan which provides a way for all of mankind to get to heaven. Simply stated, trust in what God did and do not listen to doctrines of demons.

DEALING WITH YOUR SIN NATURE

Unfortunately, all human beings are born with a sin nature, and want to appease that nature by pursuing pleasure. But running after pleasure steers us away from God's desires and brings us closer to the doors of Hell. And just in case you are one of those folks who think that Hell is just a fairy tale, there can be no doubt that Jesus believed in a literal hell, a place where the wicked and those who have no regard for God or His Word will spend eternity in torment.

Hades is pictured as a literal place where the departed believer exists in a spiritual state. Scripture likens it to being naked (2 Corinthians 5:1-10). When the Rapture occurs and Christ comes for the redeemed, they will be united with their resurrected, glorified bodies (1 Thessalonians 4:14-16). But as for the unbeliever, his or her departed spirit will go immediately to Hades to experience conscious everlasting torment.

Hell is a place of memory, continued consciousness. In the 16th chapter of Luke, Jesus tells a story about a rich man who died and went to hell. On earth, he had been indifferent to the needs of others, caring only about himself. When he opened his eyes after death, he found himself in torment. He knew who he was and why he was there, and wanted someone to go back from the dead to warn his brothers so they wouldn't wind up in this terrible place. But he was told that the only warning that would be given was the word of the prophets. If his brothers did not listen to the prophets, they would not be able to avoid this place of unquenchable fire (Luke 16:24b), a place of sorrow, anger, frustration (Matthew 13:42), a place of separation from God and unquenchable thirst.

I recently heard a story about a man—a nonbeliever--who was being treated after having a severe heart attack. For some time, the patient's life hung in balance. As the ER doctor worked on him, the heart attack victim would often clap his hands over both ears and wince. Obviously, something was bothering him that had nothing to do with the heart attack.

Finally, the man improved to the point where the doctor was able to ask him what was going on.

"It's just so loud!" he said.

"Loud?" asked the doctor. "What's loud?"

"All those people screaming," came the answer. "Can you get them to stop?"

After he recovered completely, the man didn't remember anything about the screaming. But the doctor never forgot. Could it be that the unbelieving patient was so close to Hell as he fought for his life that he heard the screams of those condemned to eternal torment? I have been told that the surgeon has since committed his life to Jesus Christ – a very wise thing for anyone to do.

DEATH IS INEVITABLE

Let's face facts. Everything dies!

If you are old, you ask, "How did I get to this age so quickly?" When you are young, you never think about age. Death is not on your radar. When it hits your friends or your family you experience the sting of death.

The sting of death is sin, and the power of sin is the law. Christ on the cross defeated sin. As Hosea 13:14 says, **"O DEATH, WHERE ARE YOUR THORNS? O SHEOL, WHERE IS YOUR STING?"**

WILL YOU CHOOSE LIFE OR DEATH?

I have heard people say, "I am a good person. I don't lie or steal, nor do I covet my neighbor's wife or possessions. Surely God cannot send me to everlasting punishment!" Anyone who believes that is essentially relying on himself or herself to get to heaven. But it can never happen that way. You cannot work yourself into heaven, and you must keep your eyes on the finished work of God, which is Jesus Christ crucified and then resurrected from the dead.

A dear woman recently told me that she doesn't need a Savior, because she has never done anything wrong. "I've been a good daughter, a good wife and a good mother," she said. "So why do I need someone to rescue me from my sins?" This lady isn't arrogant. By worldly standards, she has lived a very good life. But God's standards are not the same as the world's standards. As the apostle Paul writes in the third chapter of the book of Romans, "All have sinned and fall short of the glory of God."

In Genesis, the first book of the Bible, we learn that the first child born on the earth, Cain, made his living by working the land, growing plants and vegetables, while his brother, Abel, tended flocks of animals. In time, Cain brought some of the fruits of the land as an offering to God, while Abel brought the fat portions from some of the first-born of his flock. God accepted Able's sacrifice but rejected Cain's. Think about Cain working the land to produce crops -- a back-breaking job for sure. And yet God rejected his offering. But why? The answer is that Abel did what God asked of him, while Cain (through his own effort) thought God would appreciate all his efforts to get him to heaven.

Unfortunately for Cain--or anyone else who thinks like he did--you cannot work your way into heaven! Trust in what God has done. *You cannot add anything to the cross except your sins!*

Some folks, like our many Jewish friends, believe in God, but not Jesus. But if you read the Old Testament, you will find many prophecies about the coming of Jesus. Some scholars believe there are over 300 prophecies about Jesus in the 36 books of the Old Testament. Jesus fulfilled every one of them! Not three-fourths of them or four-fifths of them, but every one of them, the greatest being His resurrection from the dead. Jesus brings peace, joy, and most importantly, He brings purpose to your life. He raised people from the dead and performed many miracles, starting with the wedding in Cana (John 2:1-11), then the healing of a young boy in Capernaum (John 4:46-54). He walked on water and multiplied a handful of bread and some small fish to feed nearly 10,000 people.

More importantly, His 12 apostles saw Him. (Acts 1:1-22; 5:32) The facts are:

1) <u>Jesus' tomb was empty</u>. Even the Jews did not deny this fact. The stone that blocked the entrance to Jesus's tomb weighed approximately 4,000 pounds. Two strong men could get it into position to cover the entrance, but getting it away from the entrance was another story. The stone was set inside a groove in front of the entrance and secured by a stone wall that stood in front of

the tomb. In other words, you would have to roll it over and up the incline to get away from the entrance. No five men could accomplish that, and even if they could, they wouldn't be able to do it quietly. It would be a noisy, dusty process that would have attracted a lot of attention, no matter what time of day it was.

2) <u>Many, many, people wrote about the resurrection</u>. It was the most significant happening in biblical times. If it hadn't really happened, there would have been many challenges to the story from Christ's contemporaries. It would have been impossible to make up such a story and then convince people that it was true. Many people believed the disciples' claims because they were living in Jerusalem when it happened, and they remembered the buzz that had swept through the city – and the panicked cover-up instigated by the Jewish and Roman authorities. What is more, many of them had seen Jesus after His resurrection from the dead.

3) Paul provides us with a list of people whom Christ appeared to after his resurrection, starting with Mary Magdalene at the tomb (Mark 16:9), various other women (Matthew 28: 9-10), two unnamed disciples (Luke 24: 13-32), Peter and the rest of the remaining apostles (Luke: 24:36-43, John: 20: 19-25), including Thomas, who said he would not believe unless he could feel for himself the spear-wound in the Lord's side. After this, Jesus appeared to seven disciples What is at once, (John 21), and then to eleven disciples, including Peter, on a mountain in Galilee (Matthew 28:16-20). This is where Jesus told the disciples that He has been given all authority, and power. Finally, Jesus appeared to as many as 500 of His followers and assured them all that the Holy Spirit would guide them. They all then watched Jesus ascend to heaven.

You can be sure that He will return. As He said **"DO NOT LET YOUR HEART BE TROUBLED; BELIEVE IN GOD, BELIEVE ALSO IN ME. IN MY FATHER'S HOUSE ARE MANY ROOMS; IF THAT WERE NOT SO, I WOULD HAVE TOLD YOU, BECAUSE I**

AM GOING THERE TO PREPARE A PLACE FOR YOU. AND IF I GO AND PREPARE A PLACE FOR YOU, I AM COMING AGAIN AND WILL TAKE YOU TO MYSELF, SO THAT WHERE I AM, THERE YOU ALSO WILL BE (JOHN 14:1-3). *Operative words here are, "<u>I am coming again</u>."*

The question is, will you be ready?

CHAPTER NINE
THE LAND ISSUE

THE LORD SAID TO ABRAM, AFTER LOT HAD SEPARATED FROM HIM, "NOW RAISE YOUR EYES AND LOOK FROM THE PLACE WHERE YOU ARE, NORTHWARD AND SOUTHWARD, AND EASTWARD AND WESTWARD; FOR ALL THE LAND WHICH YOU SEE I WILL GIVE TO YOU AND TO YOUR DESCENDANTS FOREVER." (GENESIS 13:14-15)

Zola Levitt said it best in his book, Israel's right to the Land:[10]

"One of the central pillars of Old and New Testament is the presence of the chosen people in the Land God gave them."

In Amos 9:14-15 (KJV) the Bible says, **"AND I WILL BRING AGAIN THE CAPTIVITY OF MY PEOPLE OF ISRAEL, AND THEY SHALL BUILD THE WASTE CITIES, AND INHABIT THEM; AND THEY SHALL PLANT VINEYARDS, AND DRINK THE WINE THEREOF; THEY SHALL ALSO MAKE GARDENS, AND EAT THE FRUIT OF THEM. AND I WILL PLANT THEM UPON THEIR LAND, AND THEY SHALL NO MORE BE PULLED UP OUT OF THEIR LAND WHICH I HAVE GIVEN THEM, SAITH THE LORD THY GOD."**

[10] Levitt, Zola and Hocking, David L., "Israel's Right to the Land," (Zola Levitt Ministries; Dallas, Texas) 2024

Is what you just read taking place today? Yes, it is. The Israelis have rebuilt the cities, they are basically self-sufficient when it comes to feeding their people, and are now a world-power militarily. The Israeli "Kheil HaAvir" (Air Corps), is today recognized as one of the world's most powerful fighting forces.

As far as their over-all military power, they are ranked 18 out of 145 nations according to the Global Firepower Index.[11] Israel today is a high-tech superpower and one of the world's top exporters of weapons, with an estimated $6.5 billion in sales each year. Israel is most definitely the best friend the United States could ever have. In fact, I firmly believe that God raised up the United States to defend and protect Israel.

Many believe that the Palestinians are the rightful owners of the land on which the nation of Israel now stands. But truthfully, only God has the right to determine outcomes. God is the authority on all matters, including the most important, morality. Morality exists because God exists. As Romans 13:1-2 says, **"EVERY PERSON IS TO BE SUBJECT TO THE GOVERNING AUTHORITIES. FOR THERE IS NO AUTHORITY EXCEPT GOD, AND THOSE WHICH EXIST ARE ESTABLISHED BY GOD. THEREFORE, WHOEVER RESISTS AUTHORITY HAS OPPOSED THE ORDINANCE OF GOD; AND THEY WHO HAVE OPPOSED WILL RECEIVE CONDEMNATION UPON THEMSELVES."** The Bible does not try to prove there is a God, but rather assumes it. Pagans say there is no God. David says, **"The fool said in his heart, there is no God"** (Psalm 14:1). St. Paul wrote, **"For they exchanged the truth of God for a lie, and worshipped and served the creature rather than the Creator, Who is blessed forever." (Romans 1:25)**

---

[11] https://www. globalfirepowerindex.com: "Global Firepower – 2023 World Military Strength Rankings "

When we say that God gave the land to Israel, what land are we talking about? Genesis 15:18 tells us, **"The Lord made a covenant with Abram, saying, To your descendants I have given this land, from the river of Egypt, as far as the great river, the river Euphrates."** This is the area commonly called Canaan. The obvious question is, 'Ishmael, the father of the Arabs, is also a son of Abraham, so why does this promise not apply to the Arabs as well?" Abraham asked God the same question. In Genesis 17:19 we see God's answer. **"No! But Sarah your wife shall bear you a son, and you shall call his name Isaac; and I will establish My covenant for an everlasting covenant for his descendants after him."**

The sign of the covenant with Abraham and his descendantS was circumcision. Circumcision of the heart. In Romans 2:28 Paul writes, **"For he is not a Jew who is one outwardly, nor is circumcision that which is outward in the flesh."** In other words, God emphasizes the inward things of the heart. The Jews elevated the letter of the Law, and praise came from men. God on the other hand, cares about the spirit of the Law, and the heart. It's in the heart where we choose how we look at things. Jesus said, **"For where your treasure is, there your heart will be also"** (Matthew 6:21). He is saying that what a person values most is where their heart will be.

There are some who feel strongly that the descendants of Esau should own the land where Israel sits. They base this on the fact that Esau was manipulated by Jacob, conned may be a better word. But God reminded Moses that the land of Canaan was for Jacob and his descendants. Continuing on, we see where God tells the Israelites to conquer the land. (Deuteronomy 1:8) Joshua was placed in charge, to wipe out all the nations who lived in Canaan. This was a consequence of the wickedness of these nations, as opposed to the righteousness of Israel. It was God driving them out to confirm the oath he made with Abraham, Isaac, and Jacob. As for the sins committed by Israel, this would not affect the land as God confirmed His promise. It was their land. . . because God owned it and He gave it to them, no strings attached.

Ezekiel tells us that Jerusalem is the center of this earth. The Arabs want this Land, as do the Russians. If we look at the area God gave the Israeli nation, it takes in all the land from the Mediterranean Sea to the Euphrates River. Ezekiel fixed the northern boundary at Hamath (Ezekiel 48:1) one hundred miles north of Damascus, and the southern at Kadesh, approximately 100 miles south of Jerusalem. Had the Israelites kept the land God gave them, they would be in control of Lebanon, the West Bank plus parts of Syria, Iraq, and Saudi Arabia. My guess is that prior to the Lord's return, this land will be the same size as when God initially gave it to Israel. Sometime soon, you may see the IDF reclaim the land, by whatever means. Pray for the peace of Jerusalem.

The bottom line is that for over 3,500 years, the land belonged to Abraham, Isaac and Jacob and *their seed forever*. (Genesis 12:1-3; 13:16, 15:5, 17:7-8, 22:17-18) All the things the Lord has done, or will do, are a part of His plan to save mankind from eternal damnation.

GETTING BACK TO THE GARDEN

Ever since Adam and Eve were driven out of the Garden of Eden, every civilization has been asking how and when they can get back into Paradise. From the very beginning, mankind has looked to the Messiah to clean up the mess we made.

Starting in the days when the Old Testament was being written, man was aware of heaven, but most seemed not to care about it. God did not reveal as much about the afterlife as He did in the New Testament, but most knew that there was an opportunity for a better life after this one. The Old Testament hero Job said, **"AFTER MY SKIN HAS BEEN DESTROYED, YET IN MY FLESH I WILL SEE GOD; I MYSELF WILL SEE HIM WITH MY OWN EYES, I AND NOT ANOTHER. HOW MY HEART YEARNS WITHIN ME!" (JOB 19:26-27)** Such Old Testament saints were permitted to enter heaven when Christ preached to "the spirits in prison" (1 Peter 3:19).

How did Christ shame the devil and his cohorts? Let me set the stage; you are a witness to the activities in heaven. You initially notice, secured to a wall, humankind's record of debt. You know all mankind are born spiritually dead. In essence, man cannot hear spiritual truths. He only knows one thing and this is that his sin nature is in charge. Notice what Paul says in Colossians 2:14, God nailed the record of our debt to the cross. **"By canceling the record of debt that stood against us with its legal demands. This He set aside, nailing it to the cross."** Basically, all humans are born going to hell. We all were legally condemned because of Adam's sin. The debt owed to God would be paid by God dying and going to hell in our place. Therefore, the debt was paid, the punishment for man was given to Jesus Christ in order that we might be saved. The debt was canceled, scripture says "it was set aside" (in other words someone took it). **Psalm 103:12 says, "As far as the east is from the west, so far He removed our transgressions from us."**

When Christ died in our place, He removed the sting out of death (Hebrews 2:14). He also took condemnation out; therefore, the fear of death is removed also.

Shortly before His sacrificial death on the cross, Jesus and His disciples visited the temple, where Jesus told them that all the magnificent structures, they were looking at would be destroyed. The destruction would be so great, in fact, that not one stone would be left on top of another. Naturally, the disciples wanted to know when this terrible event would happen, and what would be the sign of Christ's return from heaven. This temple was the center of Jewish life. The Jewish historian Josephus stated that ten thousand men worked on this magnificent edifice for eight years during its destruction.

When the disciples asked Jesus what the sign of His coming would be, He gave them an interesting answer: **"SEE TO IT THAT NO ONE MISLEADS YOU. FOR MANY WILL COME IN MY NAME, SAYING, 'I AM THE CHRIST,' AND THEY WILL MISLEAD MANY PEOPLE. AND YOU WILL BE HEARING OF WARS AND RUMORS OF WARS. SEE**

THAT YOU ARE NOT ALARMED, FOR THOSE THINGS MUST TAKE PLACE, BUT THAT IS NOT YET THE END. FOR NATION WILL RISE AGAINST NATION, AND KINGDOM AGAINST KINGDOM, AND THERE WILL BE FAMINES AND EARTHQUAKES IN VARIOUS PLACES. BUT ALL THESE THINGS ARE MERELY THE BEGINNING OF BIRTH PAINS" (MATTHEW 24:4-8).

Jesus was correct ((of course) when He said that many would come in His Name, claiming to be the Christ. The list is long so I will highlight only the notables:

- **In 1600** a Welsh "prophet," named Rhys Evans was imprisoned for impersonating Christ.

- **In the 1700s,** we find Ann Lee, founder, and leader of the Shakers, who was known by her followers as "Mother." They believed she was the female incarnation of Christ.

- **About 100 years later,** 'Baha u'llah' arrived on the scene. He claimed to be the fulfillment of Hinduism, Judaism, Zoroastrianism, Buddhism, and Islam.

Then, in modern times we have had Sun Myung Moon, founder of the Unification church. You have probably seen his followers selling magazines and asking for donations at airports throughout the United States, although they are not as prevalent as they used to be. One of his big moments was when he brought thousands of men and women together in a mass wedding ceremony. Most of them had never met each other before that day.

Another who claimed to be the Messiah was David Berg (Founder of the Children of God) who taught his young female followers to become "flirty fish," using their sex appeal to bring men into his cult.

These new age gods all have one thing in common, and that is use of the use of the word "force." According to them, their god of force will unify mankind. They are driven by a desire to remove all differences and bring everything and everyone together in one world.

This is promoted by the new age movement. The Bible says, **"BUT IN HIS ESTATE SHALL HE HONOR THE GOD OF FORCES: AND A GOD HIS FATHERS KNEW NOT SHALL HE HONOR WITH GOLD, AND SILVER, AND WITH PRECIOUS STONES, AND PLEASANT THINGS" (DANIEL 11:38 KJV).** (The antichrist will take and hold power with military might and the shrewd use of money.] Keep this in mind, the greater the political upheavals, the greater the chance of nuclear war, runaway inflation, and energy crises.

As I mentioned previously, Jesus told His disciples that the temple would be destroyed and that that there would be no stone left upon another. Considering that these stones were 50 feet long, 24 feet broad and 16 feet thick according to the Antiquities of Josephus, how could this possibly happen?

Recall how this temple was constructed. According to 1 Kings chapters 4 through 10, 34 tons of gold were brought to Jerusalem from Ophir by Solomon's laborers, approximately one-half of the ancient world's supply. Then, in 70 A.D., the Romans destroyed the city. The soldiers, seeing the gold, decided to take it. They burned Jerusalem and the fire was so hot that it melted the gold, which ran into the cracks of the stones, thus allowing the soldiers the opportunity to steal the precious metal. They ransacked the temple trying to get every ounce of that gold, leaving God's house in utter ruin, just as Christ had prophesied.

The next thing Christ mentioned about the end times was that there would be wars and rumors of wars. He also told us not to worry about these battles because they are part of the normal course of events that will lead to the end times, thus fulfilling God's plan. The Bible says, **"THOUGH A HOST ENCAMP AGAINST ME, MY HEART WILL NOT FEAR; THOUGH WAR ARISE AGAINST ME, IN SPITE OF THIS I SHALL BE CONFIDENT" (PSALM 27:3).**

Wikipedia says there have been 10,624 wars since historians began counting them, and the Council on Foreign Relations says there were 32 armed conflicts raging in various parts of the globe in

2022. (According to the Institute of Economics and Peace, 238,000 people died in war that year.) But as Jesus said, "Nation will rise against nation and kingdom against kingdom and in various places there will be famines and earthquakes."

What we can say with some certainty is that Jesus died on the cross on April 3, 31 A.D. There was a major seismic event (earthquake) that day. From that point on, the number of quakes in the world seems to have rapidly grown each year. According to Encyclopedia Brittanica, there were 150 recorded earthquakes in the 15th century, 378 in the 17th century and 640 in the 18th, and those numbers have continued to increase.

Earthquakes are going up both in numbers and intensity. And yet, this is only the beginning of the terrible and painful events that will confront man in the years ahead. When the time of tribulation comes, many thousands of Christians will be killed, and all will be hated.

At this time, you will have to be tough to be a Christian. Most people are always looking for fun things to do, but God never promised us fun, He promised us peace. We are constantly reminded to 'lay up treasures in heaven,' meaning that we must believe God's promises and align yourself with other Christians as they will be afflicted as well.

"But remember the former days, when after being enlightened, you endured a great conflict of sufferings, partly by being a public spectacle through reproaches and tribulations, and partly by being sharers with those who were so treated. For you showed sympathy to the prisoners and accepted joyfully the seizure of your property, knowing that you have for yourselves a better possession and a lasting one." (Hebrews 10:32-34) Now you understand Matthew 16:24-26: ***Take up your cross and follow*** me. The person born and raised in America has no clue what 'Take up your cross' means. The short answer is that God's priorities must now be your prime focus.

When I was a young man, my prime focus was playing sports. I got my 'atta boys' from others because I was a good player. Later in life it was golf, golf, and more golf! I justified my time away from home by taking my boys with me. I coached them in their early years, and both were good athletes--but I must admit that I believe our daughter could have been the best.

Everything came natural to her. The boys were very good and all had an opportunity to play at the collegiate level, but their sister, Mary, was, in my opinion, the best athlete in the family. I was quite proud of all my children, but sad to say we were merely existing spiritually. In this regard, we were not much different from those who were alive at the time of the flood. They were eating, drinking, marrying and, basically, <u>having a good time!</u>

But we were never promised a life of fun. We are here for a reason. God has not given us a life to waste by encouraging youngsters to cross dress, or march in some pride parade, or to learn how to gain riches by cheating and lying.

If I have said this once I have said it a thousand times: God does not make mistakes! Your children were given to you because God knows you have the potential to be the best possible parents they could ever have. He calls you to teach your children to do good, to behave, to consider the other person.

So many parents today do everything they can to keep their children happy and satisfied. They give them whatever it takes to produce fewer headaches for themselves. What the children really need is time with mom and dad. They need to hear you say, "I love you." And on Sunday mornings, they need to hear you tell them to get ready for church, not "Here, take this play station and sit over there and behave."

Do you believe in God? I mean really believe? Or do you simply ascent to the idea of God? If you do believe in Him, it's important to share this information with your children. Let them know that you believe in God and tell them why. Share with them how God has made a difference in your life.

A great example of worldly wisdom came from Pope Francis when he was asked his opinion on same-sex relationships and replied, "Who am I to judge?"[12] More recently, He signaled that he is open to blessing same-sex couples, on a "pastoral" rather than official basis. I am not judging him but it sounds like Francis is "blessing" sin. God said these things are an abomination, and yet the pope is blessing them. Shame on him. His remarks have been seen by the LGBTQ+ community as a huge step in the cause of equal rights within the church. Michael Bradley of Bible-Knowledge.com wrote, "What you choose to think about and dwell on in this life will make or break you as to what type of person you will end up becoming."[13] In other words, if we spend our lives thinking about depravity and sexual sin, we will wind up as depraved men and women. We must not allow this to happen. Our lives are over in a brief second. The Bible tells us over and over to be ready for the end. Why? Because in the flash of lightning Jesus Christ will return and there will be no time to repent. Messianic Jewish Pastor Sam Nadler said it best in one of his sermons: "Isn't it better to be warned five years too soon than five minutes too late. For you don't know how soon it will be too late."

---

[12] "Who am I to judge?: The Pope's most powerful words in 2013," by Tracy Connor, Staff Writer, nbcnews.com, December 22, 2013

[13] "You Are What You Think" by Michael Bradey, bible-knowledge.com, August 8, 2023

CHAPTER TEN
RACING TOWARD THE END

The world is racing toward a cataclysm of unbelievable proportions. The greatest disaster the world has ever seen will soon unleash unprecedented terror upon this planet of ours. It will be far greater than the nuclear disaster that was unleashed on Hiroshima and Nagasaki during World War II. It will be more devastating even than the Great Flood of Noah's Day, when you consider that the world population is so much greater today.

This time around, an estimated one billion people will die. Then, Christians who remain will be delivered up to persecution. And at that time, many will fall away from the faith and will deliver up one another and hate one another. In other words, Christians should expect to be persecuted. The stage is already being set for the terrors that will fall upon those who don't escape from earth via the Rapture.

Our society today is worse than bad. It's horrendous. Blatant racism is all around us. Our politicians seem to care only about lining their pockets, so-called preachers use the word of God for personal gain, and unbridled greed has taken over where there should be love and respect. Men and women love only themselves. And what some parents and school administrators are allowing (the transgender agenda) will be on God's list of eradications.

All the lawlessness and sin that you observe today, will not stop the spread of the gospel. Jesus promised that before the end comes, the gospel will go out to all the world. Jesus also said lawlessness will increase and love will grow cold. Love grows cold because we have become so self-centered that there is no room in our hearts for anyone else.

Of course, nobody knows when the earth will take its final trip around the sun. But when the apostles asked Jesus for signs of His return, Jesus told them that the temple would be restored and that they must keep on the lookout for persecution, famines, wars, earthquakes, false prophets, and a major increase in evil. He said that tribulation would occur and that the Jews would suffer terrible, catastrophic things. He then said that we must not be led astray by false messiahs, who are basically following the demonic realm. After the tribulation, the Son of man will appear in heaven and the angels of God will gather the elect from all the earth. **"BUT OF THAT DAY AND HOUR NO ONE KNOWS, NOT EVEN THE ANGELS OF HEAVEN, NOR THE SON, BUT THE FATHER ALONE" MATTHEW 24:36).**

CONCLUSION

This recap is very simple. We must be ready at all times.

If you read this book and have not committed your life to Christ, I strongly urge you to consider whether you want to choose Christ's eternal love or Satan's temporary pleasures. Pleasures last for a few passing minutes. Love endures all, forever.

9 798990 641525